76

I
If
wil
day
bri
tel

30

31

A1

38

STILL I BELIEVE...

STILL I BELIEVE...

Nine talks broadcast during
Lent and Holy Week 1969

MALCOLM MUGGERIDGE

ANDREW CRUICKSHANK

BRONWEN ASTOR

TOM DRIBERG

QUINTIN HOGG

DAVID EDWARDS

BRITISH BROADCASTING CORPORATION

Published by the
British Broadcasting Corporation
35 Marylebone High Street
London W1M 4AA

First published 1969
© *The Contributors 1969*

Printed in England by The Broadwater Press Ltd
Welwyn Garden City, Herts.
SBN: 563 08552 5

CONTENTS

PREFACE

ALL THE talks in this booklet were broadcast on Radio 4 during Lent and Holy Week this year. The first five (printed first though they were given last) went out on the days running up to Good Friday. In them a group of laymen, notable people from several walks of life, reflect upon the events of the Passion of Jesus and say something of what those events mean to them as human beings much involved in the business of our times. No doubt all of them would agree with the words of Mr Quintin Hogg that 'something had to be done, and has to be done now, about man's lack of love for man, and because nobody else could be found to do it, God had to do it himself, in a historical context especially fashioned for the purpose, and even then it could not be done at once, but must be accomplished through the centuries, by other human beings imperfectly reflecting in their own lives the vision they themselves have seen of the figure on the cross.'

The other four talks printed here are by the Reverend David Edwards, Dean of King's College, Cambridge. He is asking if Christianity can survive in a rapidly changing world and asserts that it can, but only if Christians will preserve what is essential in their faith and let the rest go. The crux of the matter, he says, is that 'Christianity is about Christ, and if Christ were to be pushed out of his dominant position – why, then, we should need a new religion.'

At the beginning of his first talk Mr Edwards puts the question: 'Can one be modern and intelligent, *and* be on fire with faith?' The authors of this little book make it clear that one can.

JOHN LANG
Head of Religious Programmes (Radio)

FIVE HOLY WEEK TALKS

1. BEFORE THE CROSS
Malcolm Muggeridge

'WHEN I survey the wondrous cross.' The words have little meaning or significance for most people today, I know, even at Easter time. Yet I have come to love them. Of all the notions which make up the Christian faith, that of the cross seems to me the most sublime. It is the heart of the whole thing. Without the cross, there would be no Christianity. If Jesus had not died on a cross, it is extremely improbable that we should ever have heard of him, or that our civilisation would have existed at all, with its literature and its art, its saints and its mystics, its scholars and its builders, who have been the glory of the last two thousand years.

In the light of today's values, of course, the symbolism is sick. What is the cross, as my dear old agnostic father used to ask rhetorically, but a gibbet or scaffold? As it might be a hangman's rope or an executioner's block. We've done away with capital punishment, haven't we, and so surely we don't want to be reminded anymore of its gruesome accompaniments. Then again, the cross signifies sacrifice and death – two unfashionable concepts. We don't think much of sacrifice, and as for death we think even less of that, half believing that before very long medicine and surgery will abolish it altogether, as it were, keeping us on the road indefinitely, like old vintage cars whose tyres and sparking-plugs and carburettors can be replaced as and when they wear out.

The crucifixion, in any case, was in worldly terms a scene of failure and defeat, and we like success and victory. At least, the colour supplements and the television ratings say we do. A poor, crazed teacher nailed up on a cross, his few mostly illiterate followers all scattered and fled – what sort of a hero is he? A poor, crazed teacher decked out to look like a ribald King of the Jews; actually named as such on an ironical notice

7

over his stricken head. A poor, crazed teacher with some wild notion, it seems, that there would be a divine intervention on his behalf; and then, when it didn't happen, blurting out his despairing cry — 'My God, my God, why hast thou forsaken me?' After that, dying with a loud cry – 'It is finished!' But it wasn't. It was only beginning; it is not finished even yet. Witness these poor words of mine.

How not finished? Through all the intervening years Christians have believed that there was a Resurrection, that the stone in front of the tomb where Jesus was laid was pushed aside, that he rose from the dead and was seen in his mortal shape by his mother, Mary, his disciples, and numerous other persons. Much debate, some of it highly acrimonious, has arisen over the authenticity of these happenings. I can't join in – partly through ignorance, partly because for me it suffices to know that the light that Jesus shone in his lifetime continues to shine today as brightly as ever. In this sense, he is alive and accessible as, for instance, Socrates is not, who also chose to lay down his life for truth's sake.

Let the dead, as Jesus himself said, bury their dead. In other words, relate themselves to history; the living belong to life – in Jesus' case, life projected to reach beyond history into eternity. The Resurrection is historical; Jesus is truth. The cross is where history and truth, time and eternity, intersect; there Jesus is nailed forever to show us how God became a man and a man became God.

That, at least, is how I see it. The old pagan gods were all represented in terms of earthly power and wealth and physical beauty – shining and mighty and lascivious. The cross for the first time revealed God in terms of weakness and lowliness – even, humanly speaking, of absurdity. When the Roman soldiers played their sick joke on Jesus – dressing him up in a scarlet robe, putting a crown of thorns on his head, bowing low before him in mock reverence as King of the Jews – they were not, as they supposed, ridiculing a poor deluded man about to die, but all kings, all rulers, all exercisers of authority who ever had been or were to be. They were making power itself forever derisory, ensuring that thenceforth we should see thorns beneath every crown, and beneath every scarlet robe, stricken flesh. It was to be the most timid, gentle, and vulnerable of all living creatures – a lamb – that would embody the attributes of our Saviour. *Agnus Dei!* So they have been joyously singing through the centuries. *Agnus Dei!*

Standing before the cross, our defences are down, our bluff is called. There, we may understand that all power is a sham, all splendour thorns, all the claims and style of greatness so much mockery. There, we are made aware of our own nothingness. And yet God deigned to put on this nothingness, shining a very bright light in the world and showing the way to his holy city built on a hill. Standing before the cross, the world's accepted standards are turned upside down. There, we may see that it is the poor, not the rich, who are blessed; the weak, not the strong, who deserve consideration; the pure in heart, not the worldly and the sophisticated, who understand what life is about. There, God's purpose for us is blindingly clear – to love him and to love our neighbour, which means everyone without exception – so that we may be worthy members of a human family whose father is in heaven. It is on these sublime propositions, propounded by the cross, that the Christian religion is founded; if the cross has ceased to be valid, then so have they, and the long, glorious story of Christendom which began 2,000 years ago on Golgotha will be over at last.

Let me quote some words on the subject by one of the greatest Christians of modern times – the Lutheran Pastor, Dietrich Bonhoeffer:

'God's victory means our defeat, means our humiliation; it means God's mocking anger at all human arrogance, being puffed up, trying to be important in our own right. It means reducing the world and its clamour to silence; it means the crossing through of all ideas and plans, it means the cross. The cross above the world. It means that man, even the noblest, must, whether he likes it or not, fall in the dust and with him all gods and idols and lords of this world. The cross of Jesus Christ, that means the bitter scorn of God for all human heights, bitter suffering of God in all human depths, the rule of God over the whole world.'

Bonhoeffer's views on the cross, as we know, were put to the supreme test; he was subjected to the agony, and accorded the high privilege of following his Master's example and himself dying for the light he had seen and the truth he had proclaimed. How superbly his faith stood up to the test! With what a shining joy he confronted, as he put it, an end which was also a beginning! A fellow-prisoner, an Englishman named Payne Best who was with him at the time, has described the scene.

Bonhoeffer was asked to hold a service, but as most of his companions were Roman Catholics, and one of them – Kokorin, a Russian – was a Communist, he hesitated. They were insistent, especially Kokorin. Ecumenicalism indeed! Bonhoeffer took as his text Isaiah 53:5, 'Through his stripes we are healed,' and 1 Peter 1:3, 'Blessed be the God and Father of our Lord Jesus Christ, which according to his abundant mercy hath begotten us again into a lively hope of the resurrection of Jesus Christ from the dead.' 'He reached the hearts of all,' Payne Best recalled afterwards, 'finding just the right words to express the spirit of our imprisonment, and the thoughts and resolutions which it had brought.' Together with Bonhoeffer they all looked forward thankfully and hopefully into the future.

Almost as soon as the little service was over, two men came for Bonhoeffer and took him away. Before he went, he sent, through Payne Best, a message for his friend Dr Bell, Bishop of Chichester – 'Tell him that with him I believe in the principle of our universal Christian brotherhood which rises above all national interests, and that our victory is certain.' Later, a prison doctor caught a glimpse of him after he had been condemned to die; still wearing his prison clothes, he was kneeling in fervent prayer to the Lord his God. 'The devotion and evident conviction of being heard, that I saw in the prayer of this intensely captivating man,' the doctor has recalled, 'moved me to the depths.' The next morning Bonhoeffer was ordered to strip and taken to the place of execution. 'Naked under the scaffold in the sweet spring woods, he knelt for the last time to pray. Five minutes later, he too gave up the ghost.'

This scene (for which, incidentally, I am indebted to Mary Bosanquet's splendid biographical study of Bonhoeffer which everyone should read) perfectly conveys what I think the cross signifies. Like the scene on Golgotha from which it derives, it should be seen in its historical setting. The time was April 1945; five years of war's murderous buffooneries were drawing to a close. Hitler's Reich that was to last a thousand years would soon reach its destructive and ignominious end; the liberators were moving in from the east and the west with bombs and tanks and guns and cigarettes and spam; the air was thick with rhetoric and cant.

Looking back now in April 1969, on that other April twenty-four years ago, I ask myself where in the murky darkness any light shone. Not among the Nazis, certainly, or among the liberators, who, as we well know, liberated no one and nothing. The rhetoric and the cant are mercifully forgotten; what lives on is the memory of a man who died, not on behalf of freedom or democracy or any other of the twentieth century's counterfeit hopes, but of the cross, the wondrous cross.

2. THE LONELY SELF

Andrew Cruickshank

CHRIST'S SIN lay in his life, a life that was lived continuously towards others, and for others, without discrimination or resentment. He proceeded by teaching men and women a way to freedom until that moment when those responsible for the security of the Jewish state recognised his teaching as a challenge to their authority. Did authority lie in a state that claimed a unique covenant with God, or could a man derive his authority directly from God? Once the crisis had been exposed, what followed is familiar. The journey to Jerusalem, the last supper with the disciples, the ordeal in Gethsemane of recognising the nature of his authority, his abandonment by the disciples, his denial by Peter, his trial and conviction. And finally, his crucifixion between two robbers, for it could be predicted by anyone corroded with conformity that such a man would be reckoned among criminals, and his absolute acceptance of solitude and anonymity. The pattern of Christ's life reaches its climax in his acceptance of solitude, and the consequences of that solitude.

For me the central message of the crucifixion and therefore the central message of the New Testament is the news of God's abandonment of man – no, not man, God's abandonment of a person. And we have it on the very best authority, we have God's own word for it.

Someone has described these last words that the Christian hears from the cross as God speaking to himself. Am I then trespassing when I listen to them? No, I am here at the crucifixion by invitation. I have been invited by one who said 'Come unto me all you who labour and are heavy laden, and I will refresh you.' I have come by invitation, in the same way, in precisely the same way, that every other single person in the world can be here alone, the lonely self before another lonely self. And I must listen alone.

The Church has no sacrament for Good Friday; it has no ritual for the last words from the cross. Indeed, I must confess with some humility that, far from being an illumination, the Church and its clergy have often seen the crucifixion and the last words as a source of embarrassment to be passed over as quickly as possible. 'It's dicey,' a clergyman said to me recently.

Dicey – and dangerous. Listen. I am amazed as I hear the first cry. I say to myself that I can't be hearing correctly. And yet I must be. It is the one cry from the cross that is reported by two of the evangelists, by Mark and Matthew. It is the one cry of the cross that is repeated in its original mixture of Hebrew and Aramaic. In all the gospels that have been translated into the hundreds of languages these words have been repeated in the original.

They are, 'Eli, Eli, lama sabachthani,' which means, 'My God, my God, why have you abandoned me?' How can I make sense of that? I understand the words, but what do they mean? Is it this? By taking this suffering upon himself Christ renounced the world and God in order to be freely himself. Is it possible that at the moment of death when one would expect Christ to resign himself to the blessedness of God's cause, just then comes the assertion of solitude, an assertion so painful that it encompasses all suffering yet proclaims the right of all men that through Christ on the cross each man can be free? The complete humanity of the man Jesus as he hangs on the cross is proclaimed as we hear the first cry, 'My God, my God, why have you abandoned me?' This situation all men must live through if they are to understand the suffering involved in being a free man, and what it means that others are free.

In the silence of these three days between Maundy Thursday and Easter Sunday, I think we must see and understand, as Kierkegaard understood, that suffering is the sign of the relation to God, is the love of God. Simeon saw this when he blessed the child Jesus. He turned to Mary and said, 'This shall be a sign that men shall reject. Yea, and a sword shall pierce thy heart also.' So wherever suffering happens in the world, wherever a man or woman is affronted and abandoned, then like Mary our heart is pierced.

Two things can happen when the heart is pierced. A man can shrivel; if not physically, then he can wilt away in sadness as he withdraws from the world and loses touch with life, as he withdraws into himself and the illusions of his own security. On the other hand the heart can be so pierced that it is open, open to respond to the most delicate suffering, and then the pierced heart is the most creative element in life. But there is a sort of suffering which is self-pity and protects one from life. Pascal tells us that it is so difficult to believe because it is so difficult to suffer.

No, no; we must go forward as Christ in his suffering goes forward. For if 'My God, my God, why have you abandoned me?' is the first cry from the cross, it is not the last. As we peer at the cross and wonder at the first words which would seem to contradict everything he had lived for, we listen to Luke. And I think Luke is trying to tell us that precisely at that moment at which Christ proclaimed his humanity he cried again, and said, 'Father, into thy hands I commit my spirit.' Men have died in silence and despair, men have died cursing God, men have died in fear and trembling; but I wonder if any man ever died in such command over himself in the most painful circumstances that he could commit himself outwards to another. Trust, reconciliation, love. If God so loved the world that he gave his only begotten Son that we should not perish but have everlasting life, how otherwise could the gift be sealed into a mortal passing life? 'My God, my God, why have you abandoned me.' 'Father into Thy hands I commit my spirit.'

A man reconciles himself to his abandonment by God and the world, by moving outwards towards God and the world. There is no moment in the New Testament when the man Jesus is not aware of himself and what he is doing. Even now at the point of death he is securely in charge of himself. In this lies the Christian pattern of life. For this is the total message of the crucifixion and Good Friday: that as Christ forgave those who tried and condemned him, as he comforted those who hung by his side, as he recognised his mother and drew inwards in his thirst and agony, he reached that moment of self-revelation which is the moment when all men are revealed to themselves in solitude. This is where a man starts because no one else can do this for him. I think that we Christians are to blame by our failure to live continually in the light of the central message of the crucifixion. If we are to start again, it is now, at this moment; there is no putting this off to a more convenient time when perhaps we will be more prepared.

A man is free. Free to live away from himself towards others and the world. Towards his wife, his children, his colleagues, his neighbours, his country, his world, his universe. I don't think Paul knew about the last words from the cross; certainly he never used them. But he did grasp what it was all about, as we know from his letter to the Galatians, where he tells us, 'But God forbid I should boast of anything save the cross of our Lord, Jesus Christ, through which the world is crucified to me, and I to the world.'

There is grace about Paul's words for he, like us, has been invited and stands before the cross and, while accepting the invitation, has heard the words that follow: 'For my yoke is easy, and my burden is light.'

Truly, the Christian style of life is that while the heart is pierced and open the life is buoyant, directed always outwards; 'Into your hands I commit my spirit.'

I suppose it is only at this time of the year that one can talk like this, and there is a sense in which I have not been talking at all. It would be more accurate to say that I have been thinking aloud, and indeed in this place where I am, I am alone. And now I begin to understand the reticence and discretion of the Church during these three days. I think it lies in the recognition that what was unspeakable has been given expression. A secret has been vouchsafed to us, and we must treasure it, that on Good Friday God did not deem it above himself to be reckoned among criminals.

For years I was puzzled by a strange omission in the Resurrection literature. I used to wonder why the evangelists with their great sensibility did not tell us of Jesus appearing to his mother. It seemed to me that of all those who were alive on that day when they crucified her Lord she would need his assurance. Now, I see it rather differently – Mary was silent; she dared still to believe, she was still humble enough to believe, that she was in truth the chosen among women. This Mary took upon herself. For she had found grace in the sight of God. Her heart had been pierced, and she was silent.

On Good Friday I think a man might find in his solitude before the suffering on the cross that his heart was pierced and open to the sure knowledge that the only thing that matters is new creation.

3. TO LOVE IS TO DIE
Bronwen Astor

FOR ME to live is to love. To love is to die; to keep dying to the self. To die can be to live again – to live for God.

I think to live *is* to love, for one is only alive when one is loving. In saying one is alive I mean that one's spirit is alive: when I love I feel totally aware – conscious – living within a fourth dimension that seems to make everything far more significant. Imagine feeling this not just towards the few people one loves but to everyone. This sort of love is perfect love and a sacrifice of the self.

St Paul tells us in the famous passage in Corinthians that

'love is patient; love is kind and envies no one. Love is never boastful nor conceited, nor rude; never selfish, not quick to take offence. Love keeps no score of wrongs; does not gloat over other men's sins but delights in the truth. There is nothing love cannot face; there is no limit to its faith, its hope, and its endurance.'

And in Matthew 10:37–9 we are told by Christ:

'Anyone who prefers father or mother to me is not worthy of me. Anyone who prefers son or daughter to me is not worthy of me. Anyone who does not take his cross and follow in my footsteps is not worthy of me. Anyone who finds his life will lose it; anyone who loses his life for my sake will find it.'

The thing is that those who have really learned to love God have found that they love other people more and more, because loving God to this degree results in perfect freedom in our love of husband, son, and daughter; for what we love is the total person, the God in them. We are linked to them soul to soul, centre to centre. I have discovered that the Christ in me is linked inexorably to the Christ in every other human being.

Love of this sort survives everything, even death. I would even go so far as to say *only* love survives total death.

In my own experience I have found that to live an unloving life results in aridity all around one. One is unproductive, unfruitful, relationships are sour, nothing prospers. We are all looking for love – for union – and what do we usually do? We look to be loved *by* someone. I think this is a great mistake we make. It is an understandable one; for however much my parents loved me, I still went on longing for perfect love from another human being. And then one day I discovered God loved me more than any human being could possibly do. I stopped looking for someone to love me and found plenty of people needing my love. It is said to be a woman's nature to love; that we don't necessarily have to have been loved to be able to love another. We've all of us known women capable of a wonderful unpossessive love. You see it often in nurses or in mothers. But often one doesn't face up to the suffering involved in this sort of loving. Because it does mean getting hurt. One is so frightfully vulnerable, so we shirk it. And yet I'm sure that unless, say, a mother can give enough love to her son, he will never know how to give it when he's grown up.

And to give out love, to love continually no matter how one is treated in return, this involves suffering, dying to the self; even, in extreme cases, literally dying. So we live, if we love, continually dying. For the Christian soul there is no fear of death, because he himself has been dying all through life. But we have to learn to do this. It is like an athlete's training. It means a constant discipline in all the little things. This involves the will and we have free will: to will one's self to love others, to bend one's will to the will of God. I'd say will-power is the key to the problem. To develop this strength of will at first takes a tremendous effort, but after this initial effort, which is the hardest part, we suddenly discover God's love for us, coming back through other people; and it's not always coming from the person we love but from another direction. So it gathers momentum. The love in our soul grows and strengthens the will to love more, the selfish character slowly dies in us, the spiritual character grows. The Christian recognises this (St Paul again) when he says, 'Not I but Christ in me.' This, to me, is an extraordinary and very reassuring fact.

In Holy Week I am particularly conscious of the supreme example of all this. Christ's death was the perfect act of love because it was a giving of himself. It was an act of the will; he willed his death. He let others put him to death. He need not have walked into Jerusalem in the first place. He knew what he was doing. It was the complete manifestation of his obedience to God, to the law of love. He had to face a terrible death. His wisdom as the Son of God was not enough. All the acts of healing and miracles that he had performed could not measure up to this final act of death. In this death we can identify ourselves with him.

For I believe that the final decision for each of us for or against God awaits us at the moment of death, and that even an infant, or a mentally defective, freed from the body, makes this decision.

I've been reading a book called *The Moment of Truth* by Ladislaus Boros. He says that when we die: 'The soul's freeing from the body in death does not just mean a withdrawal from matter. Rather does it signify the entering into a closer proximity with matter.' So Christ, on his death, plunged as a human into the heart of the universe. Boros goes on to say that

'He penetrated the very depths of matter, into the interior of everything. We call this hell. But hell is not a place—there is not the same time, space, and place outside this world. Hell is a process. The process is our encounter with God who is at the heart of things. At the heart of time and space.'

The Gospels tell us that the earth turned dark on that first Good Friday. And there was an earthquake. And a small crack appeared in the ground, splitting the rock of Golgotha, running through the gate of Jerusalem, through the town and the Jewish Temple, splitting the veil of the Temple, a great tapestry that would take ten men to lift, hanging in front of the Holy of Holies – splitting this veil in two, from top to bottom.

To cite Ladislaus Boros again:

'This veil was torn in two at Christ's death to show us that, at the moment when Christ's act of redemption is consummated, the whole cosmos opens itself to the Godhead, bursts open for God like a flower bud. In his triumphant descent into the innermost fastnesses of the world, the Son of God tore open the whole world and made it transparent to God's light: nay, he made of it a vehicle of sanctification. In that moment, the movement that had been going on for thousands of millions of years, the sighing and groaning of creation reached their end. The universe is no longer what it was before.'

After his death and his descent into the heart of the universe, Christ came back to tell us what he had done. As I see it, on that glorious Easter Sunday there came a turning point in time. He had entered the realm of the spirit.

Easter Day was the first day of the new *now*: the new time. Christ had broken through to the last day. And in this realm of the spirit Christ can exist everywhere and be in contact with all men of all ages in all time. Which is why it becomes for me such an intimate and personal relationship. Christ really can exist in my body, nurtured by every meal I take and every act I commit.

There was no Christianity until after the first Pentecost – when the risen Christ sent the Holy Spirit as he had promised to do, to give supernatural powers to those ordinary fishermen and tax-collectors. I am perfectly certain this supernatural power is as much in the world today as it was 2,000 years ago.

What Christ went through we too must go through, and in going through these same processes of love and death we encounter him at every moment. Because there is nowhere he has not already penetrated, he is everywhere and in everything.

Finally, as a woman, I want to say this: I believe that God created the perfect woman, who would be capable of bearing his Son. He created her. He then asked her a question. He asks us the same question all the time. It is something like this: 'Are you willing to take up the Cross of Love? It will not bring earthly pleasure, but true happiness.'

'Yes,' said Mary, 'be it done unto me, according to thy word.' I know it didn't take the form of a question in the Bible; it reads more like a statement of fact. The angel appeared to her and told her what was God's will for her, and she accepted it. We probably would have said that either we couldn't face it, or we'd have to think about it, or we're unworthy of it; but she said none of these things. It was her purity of obedience and chastity that drew God into the world. And if we women lose this, are we perhaps letting down humanity? There is not much store put on chastity at the moment. Today it is unfashionable. But haven't we, nearly all of us, at the back of our minds the instinct to preserve it; the realisation that it's a quality of cosmic proportions, through which God acts?

Of course, none of us is as pure as Mary was, or even Bernadette of Lourdes or Little Thérèse of Lisieux. But for the Christian there is always a way back to purity by means of confession and forgiveness, the opportunity to try again and again and again. Confession and prayer strengthen the will. They help to bend our will to the will of God; to fix our will-power on loving, and enduring all the suffering that loving entails, to the death of the self, even to death itself.

And so I believe we are living through dying. We live to die to rise again to love. We are told that Mary was there at her Son's death standing by the cross. He said to her, 'Woman behold your son' and to St John, 'Behold your mother.' Symbolically, she was given the whole world to mother. So I too must love her, and give her her rightful place in the history of the human spirit, and as I come to see her more and more as the greatest example of human love that a human soul can bear, I can meditate with my Roman brothers and sisters on the words of the Angel Gabriel:

'Hail Mary, full of grace! the Lord is with thee; blessed art thou amongst women, and blessed is the fruit of thy womb, Jesus. Holy Mary, mother of God, pray for us sinners, now and at the hour of our death.'

4. THE COMMON MEAL
Tom Driberg

WHEN WE are going on a long journey, and want to say good-bye to our closest friends, we probably have a party with them; maybe a tea-party, or we might all have supper together.

The day before Jesus took the longest journey that anyone can take – the journey into death – he and his friends gathered for supper; and because it was just before his arrest and execution, it has always been called the Last Supper. The rest of them did not realise what was going to happen, but they must have had a sense of foreboding; for he was saying some rather odd things – making mysterious and uncomfortable remarks, not exactly what some people would consider to be in good taste on such an occasion.

For despite the sadness of the parting of which he warned them, it was a sort of feast, too. There was a Jewish festival, the festival of Passover and unleavened bread, and on his instructions they had made careful preparations for it and had booked a private room, upstairs – above some sort of café, I suppose – and had made sure that the food and the wine had been laid on.

But there he was, almost as soon as they had all sat down, saying this very awkward thing: 'I tell you this: one of you will betray me – one who is eating with me.' Naturally, they were shocked and upset, and started asking whom he meant. This incident is described, in slightly differing ways, in all four Gospels. I think the ominous atmosphere created by this strange, apparently rather anti-social, remark is best conveyed in the *New English Bible* translation of St John's Gospel (John 13:21–30):

'After saying this, Jesus exclaimed in deep agitation of spirit, "In truth, in very truth I tell you, one of you is going to betray me." The disciples looked at one another in bewilderment: whom could he be speaking of? One of them, the disciple he loved, was reclining close beside Jesus. So Simon Peter nodded to him and said, "Ask who it is he means." That disciple, as he reclined, leaned back close to Jesus and asked, "Lord, who is it?" Jesus replied, "It is the man to whom I give this piece of bread when I have dipped it in the dish." Then, after dipping it in the dish, he took it out and gave it to Judas, son of Simon Iscariot. As soon as Judas had received it Satan entered him. Jesus said to him, "Do quickly what you have to do." No one at the table understood what he meant by this. Some supposed that, as Judas was in charge of the common purse, Jesus was telling him to buy what was needed for the festival, or to make some gift to the poor. Judas, then, received the bread and went out. It was night.'

One thing that strikes me about this account is that, having made that accusing remark, and having stirred up all that excitement and curiosity, Jesus still doesn't *openly* denounce Judas by name – either through tact (because it really would have broken up the party to do so) or through pity for what his betrayer must have been feeling, or perhaps because he knew that he had to go through with what was coming to him and that Judas was the informer who had to 'do quickly' what he had to do.

It is impossible to get to the bottom of this whole episode – or indeed fully to understand the other thing that Jesus is recorded as saying. He took bread, and having said the blessing – a Jewish custom, I suppose, what we might call 'saying grace' – he broke the bread and handed it round to his friends, saying, 'Take this and eat: this is my body.' Then he poured a cupful of wine, and said, 'This is my blood shed for many for the remission of sins.' Some witnessses added later that he had also said: 'Do this as a memorial of me.'

Whatever he meant by these words – and his followers down the centuries have interpreted them in various ways – these same phrases will be recited, in hundreds of different languages, in many thousands of churches throughout the world on Maundy Thursday. That Last Supper is then re-enacted, as it is also re-enacted every Sunday; because the re-enacting of this farewell party of Jesus and his friends has become the central act of worship of the Christian Church.

There are several things about the original Supper that seem worth noting (if we can assume that the Gospel records are fairly correct, and they are the only records of it that we have and don't vary a great deal, except in minor details).

First, those who took part in it were themselves doing what we do every time we are present at our memorial of it, whether we call it the Lord's Supper, Holy Communion, the Eucharist, or the Mass: they too were re-enacting an ancient drama, reminding themselves of their forefathers' history. In their Passover, their paschal feast, the Jews recalled the Exodus, their going out from slavery in Egypt, when they were sustained on the way to freedom by eating the paschal lamb. So Christians believe that, with Jesus as the new paschal lamb, feeding them with his own body and blood – the body that was to be broken, the blood that was to be shed, the very next day – each re-enactment of that scene in the upper room is both sacrificial and liberating: his the sacrifice, ours the liberation.

Secondly, the informer Judas was still among them at the table when Jesus distributed the bread and the wine that he had blessed. It seems to be part of the universal human experience that there should always be a traitor at the feast. But none of us can be sure that even the worst traitor is finally done for: maybe 'between the saddle and the ground he mercy sought and mercy found.' I certainly hope so; for there is a bit of Judas in every one of us – even when we kneel at the altar rail – and much more when we act or think meanly, with less than total love, of any of our fellow human beings.

Because this is the real meaning of the whole episode. Only St John's Gospel brings it out fully. It may be significant that this account does not mention the momentous central action, the distribution of the blessed bread and wine. Instead, it records at some length the other things that Christ said – the same things that he had demonstrated, perhaps for the simpler of them, with the bread and the wine: words about peace, 'Set your troubled hearts at rest'; and about the clash with a wicked social order that they would be involved in; and, above all, his 'new commandment': 'Love one another.'

The food served at that supper, like most things we eat and drink today, was not, strictly speaking, natural. The corn and the grapes were products of nature – gifts of God, if you like.

But bread and wine were made by men, men co-operating in hard work. So the bread and wine offered, blessed, and broken on Maundy Thursday and every Sunday, represent all our bread, all our work, given and enjoyed in a common meal. As William Temple put it: 'We bring familiar forms of economic wealth, which is always the product of man's labour exercised upon God's gifts, and offer them as symbols of our earthly life.'

For the Communion service, you see, is not a private devotion: it is essentially social and corporate. Here is William Temple again: 'It is the family meal where the children gather round the table to receive what the father gives them.' And what he gives them is a material gift – bread and wine – for Christianity is a materialist rather than a purely spiritual or other-worldly religion. 'The bread of the sacrament stands for all bread and ultimately for all nature.' The sacramental principle means that real values are conveyed through material objects and experiences – bread, wine, water, the touch of a hand, a lover's kiss. (But it should never be the kiss of Judas.)

Finally, a nice touch: the Gospels tell us that when they had finished supper, and no doubt recovered from the shock they had had – the wine may have helped – they sang a hymn, the Passover hymn. I like hymns very much. Some of the finest of our hymns are those which relate to this evening's events and the Eucharist which has perpetuated them for 2,000 years. The best of all, I think, is a medieval hymn which is translated:

'The Word of God proceeding forth,
Yet leaving not his Father's side,
And going to his work on earth,
Had reached at length life's eventide.'

And then one verse, verse three, says a lot, very compactly:

'In birth man's fellow-man was he,
His meat while sitting at the board:
He died, his ransomer to be;
He reigns to be his great reward.'

Of course, it wasn't really, after all, the *last* supper of Jesus and his friends. He met them again some days later, after he had been through his supreme ordeal; perhaps because of this, they didn't recognise him at first – until they sat down to a meal together, and he broke bread and *then* they knew who he was.

But that is another story: the Easter story.

5. THE SHORTEST WAY HOME
Quintin Hogg

WHATEVER MAY have happened on Easter Morning, there can
be no doubt at all as to what happened on Good Friday. And
whether we have religious convictions or not, it is as well to
remind ourselves for a moment what a grisly business it must
have been.

Crucifixion was a vile punishment, introduced as a general
method of execution, it is said, by the Macedonians after
Alexander's conquests. However that may have been, the
Romans adopted it as a common way of executing slaves or
citizens of subject nations. As many as 1,000 slaves on crosses
lined one of the main highways out of Rome when they put
down one of their rebellions at the end of the republican
period. And although the Jews detested crucifixion as uniquely
defiling, the sight of crosses outside the city wall of Jerusalem
can have been no uncommon spectacle when Pontius Pilate
was Governor of Judaea nearly 100 years later.

The constant appearance of the crucifix in Christian art
should not blind us to the innate frightfulness of the process.
It involved one of the most protracted and agonising deaths,
all the more horrible because it was public, none the less painful because it was prolonged, the victim unable to move his
pain-racked arms even to brush away the flies which settled
constantly upon his sweating face. You remember that, after
Jesus had been on the cross for three hours, the centurion
broke the legs of the two thieves, who were presumably still
alive, and pushed a spear into Jesus' side, to make sure that all
three were dead before they came down. Three hours was a
quite unusually short time for a victim to linger.

The cross was not at all as high as it is often painted. It
would not have stood up under the weight of a man if it had
been as high as all that. You could have touched the victim's
feet if the guards had let you, and, if you had tipped them, they
would have let you get close enough to press a sponge close to
his lips at the end of a short stick or a reed from the river.

The suffering of Jesus was cut short by the treatment to which he had been subjected since the night before: the midnight trial, the flogging with the terrible Roman cat, sufficient in itself to induce a state of prostration and shock, a black eye from one of Herod's soldiers, and a fool's cap of thorns pushed down on his head by the Roman detachment playing their own peculiar game of noughts and crosses on the pavement outside the Governor's residence. The cap of thorns, I am told, was the customary reward of the loser. Then came the long walk bearing the cross-piece of the cross itself (the upright would probably have already been on site), the shock of the nails driven through the wrists and ankles, and finally the helpless agony of exposure to which there could only be one end, an end passionately desired, but so long, so cruelly long, in coming before the victim could truthfully say, 'It is finished.'

Eli, Eli, lama sabachthani?

My God, my God, why hast thou forsaken me?

What kind of a man was he from whose lips was forced the despairing cry from the twenty-second psalm? Not the brutalised criminal accustomed to violence and used to ill treatment in return. The same lips had once said, 'Blessed are the meek,' 'Blessed are the poor in spirit,' 'Blessed are they that hunger and thirst after righteousness,' and 'Blessed are the pure in heart, for they shall see God.' He was pure enough in heart, but he felt himself forsaken by God. He thirsted, but his thirst was not slaked even by the sponge of vinegar.

Perhaps we make too much of his innocence, innocent as he was. The full horror of the occasion is realised when we understand that, quite apart from his goodness, Jesus was a gay person who loved this life and did not wish to die. He was full of laughter and fun. He delighted in the companionship of men and women. He was fond of anecdotes, called his friends by pet names. He was quick and genial, humorous and sensitive. The man on the cross was not a frightening figure, no *Christos Pantocrator*, no ascetic Elijah from the wilderness wearing a hair shirt. He was a warm figure of flesh and blood, criticised by his enemies as a winebibber, a frequenter of bad company.

The man they crucified was probably the best dinner companion who ever lived.

Good Friday means different things to different people. Its lesson is inexhaustible. So the three short things that I shall say are by no means the only, or perhaps the most important, things to say about it.

When Clovis the Frank was told the tale, his immediate reaction was that if he had been there with his soldiers he would never have allowed it to happen. But Jesus believed that, even without Clovis, he could have had soldiers enough, if he had wanted. If he had wanted, there would have been no Christianity today. 'My Kingdom is not of this world, else would my servants fight.' But his purpose was to identify and promote the religion of love. The movement he founded to embody this religion owes its origin to his death, and could have had no existence apart from that. This purpose, with its consequence, is the only thing which marks this crucifixion out from the tens of thousands of other victims, innocent and guilty, who met their death in this way under Roman rule. It was an end foreseen but not desired, though, in a sense, chosen. Only so could the religion of love be established among men. It was the last but necessary resort for a man who loved his life and did not wish to die.

To this day, people write ingenious and learned books as to who was to blame for the crucifixion. Rome? Pilate? The Jews? Caiaphas? Judas Iscariot? Until recently, innocent Jewish people, who had as little to do with the crucifixion as you or I, have been persecuted by Christians as deicides, murderers of God, as if Jesus' dying prayer, 'Forgive them for they know not what they do,' had never been uttered even of those who were really guilty of the crime.

As little to do with the crucifixion as you or I? That, surely, is the point. There is a sense, not merely mawkish or mystical, in which each one of us did crucify Christ. There was none other good enough. It a is great mistake to look for scapegoats in this matter – except perhaps in the looking-glass. Whatever else the atonement means, it does not mean that somebody had to be punished to appease God for something someone else had done, still less that somebody ought to be punished now. It means that something had to be done, and has to be done now, about man's lack of love for man, and because nobody else could be found to do it, God had to do it himself, in a historical context especially fashioned for the purpose, and even then it could not be done at once, but must be accomplished through the centuries, by other human beings imperfectly reflecting in their own lives the vision they themselves have seen of the figure on the cross. But for him, there would have been no focus for the religion of love. The religion of exploitation, of punishment, of self-interest, is too strong to be beaten by the meek and yielding spirit of love in the absence of this compelling figure of sacrifice, dying then, but alive now on earth and present in his servants to this day.

What I want to say can be summed up in a very few sentences. We hear a lot nowadays about demonstrations against this or that. Though some are factitious or trivial, many reflect a genuine wrong or injustice. But such demonstrations, based on hatred, even of something or someone intrinsically and genuinely evil, are in themselves simply examples of the fatuity of seeking to cast out Satan by invoking Beelzebub. Whatever the cause, the religion of hatred is not the way to destroy injustice. The longest way round is the shortest way home, and the way of love is desperately long and stony in all conscience.

There are others in the contemporary world who think they can opt out of the plight of humanity. So they opt out – or so they think. Drink, drugs, sex, tv, even literature, art, or the esoteric coterie, all well enough in their way, can all become escape hatches to withdraw or disconnect from life. It may seem an impossible task to go on living and loving in the face of poverty, disease, ignorance, squalor, filth, cruelty, and war, to improve things by the force of love, act by act, step by step, here a little and there a little, dedicated life by dedicated life, generation after generation. After 2,000 years progress seems, it may be, little enough. But the figure on the cross urges us on

inexorably and mercilessly. 'My kingdom is not of this world.'
'Love your enemies.' 'Do good to them that persecute you.'
'Your sins of omission are as bad as your sins of commission.'
'In as much as ye did it not unto one of the least of these my
little ones, ye did it not unto me.' Which of us can look into
those dying eyes and live only unto himself?

We are often told that Christianity is irrelevant. Of course
it is relevant. The question is whether it is true. Whether it is
true depends on what may have happened on Easter morning.
But its relevance depends on what did happen on Good
Friday.

For it is we who are tempted to despair when we look at the
mess of our own lives, the complexities of human life in
general, the disasters, natural and artificial, which have to be
coped with, the cruelty, the misery, the sheer silliness. It is we
who are tempted to say, 'My God, my God, why hast thou
forsaken us?'

We have lost God – or so we think. He has forsaken us
indeed, or so it seems. We cannot find him anymore, any-
where – look as we may. The world is meaningless and bad, or
meaningless and to be borne, that is, Jack, if I'm all right. But
see there he is, the God whom we thought we had lost,
revealed in a pitiful human figure, exposed for public ridicule
upon a gibbet.

And if we despair of man, look up, behold again the same
figure – God, judge, advocate, and friend – enthroned in
majesty on the right hand of power. In this sign shalt thou
conquer. The sign of Calvary, which greeted Constantine at
the Milvian bridge, is ours today if we wish it and, as it did to
Constantine, promises victory for the morrow.

But remember, it is a sign of pain and sacrifice. That is what
gives it its meaning.

CHRISTIANITY IN A CHANGING WORLD

by David Edwards

I. FAITH IN AN AGE OF MATERIALISM

IT IS, I think, very difficult to be a Christian in Britain today. I don't mean only that it is difficult to arouse much enthusiasm for the churches as they are. We all know that the British churches are confused and depressed, and in need of a radical renewal. But in this talk, I want to concentrate on the basic difficulty confronting the churches, which is that many people find it difficult to think honestly and sincerely that Christianity is essentially true. I am sure that the question which is crucial for the future of Christianity is: Can one be modern and intelligent, *and* be on fire with faith?

I don't think that this widespread suspicion of religious faith results mainly from the victory of science over religion. Of course, I know that many beliefs which used to be taught by the churches – and which still are taught by some fundamentalists – have been shown to be untrue by the scientific study of nature, or by the scientific study of history. But I don't think that many people do believe that science has displaced religion in the field where religion rightly belongs. Not many of us are expert scientists. And another fact about our situation is that the best scientists are often also the most modest. They are not the ones who talk vaguely about the scientist replacing God. They are the first to tell us that the really big questions – ultimate questions about the meaning of human life in this stupendous universe, or even immediate questions such as whether to drop a bomb on a city – just cannot be answered by using scientific methods.

I think that the real difficulty for religion comes because our age is an age of materialism. Among intellectuals – who are, of course, only a minority in any society – the trend has been to concentrate on the things which can be investigated precisely, to reduce life to what you can touch and see. Scientists have concentrated on physics and chemistry, and have not given the same energy to the far more complicated problems of human life in society. Philosophers, at least in Britain, have concentrated on the analysis of our everyday talk, and have on the whole avoided the larger mysteries. This intellectual trend has corresponded with the popular attitude that it is sensible to concentrate on money and fun. Your standard of living means your pay packet, not your spiritual wisdom. Progress means technological progress, not a deeper insight. It is also sensible to enjoy friendship or marriage or art or music; but don't think that those pleasures provide any kind of trustworthy clue in answering the ultimate questions about human destiny. The ultimate questions can't be answered and aren't worth asking. This attitude, shared basically by intellectuals and ordinary people alike, is called 'being realistic'. I frankly think it is materialism. And I think it has been attractive because, in Britain in our time, so many people are enjoying the good material things of life as their parents could not enjoy them. We are a newly rich society – and therefore a materialistic one.

Why don't I share this attitude? I'm probably as cynical and as selfish as anyone else, so it's not a heavenly-minded holiness that sets me in the minority, against the stream. No, two great things have influenced me.

It is part of my present business in a university to read and think about religious and spiritual history. From my study of history I know that religion has been at the heart of the story of mankind, until the end of the seventeenth century at least. Men and women have united their societies around a religious vision of life and, as individuals, they have been most creative and most noble when they thought that they were being obedient to the religious vision. It just isn't fair to emphasise only the cruelty which has gone on in the name of religion, or only the superstition, without admitting the massive fact of religion's enrichment of human life.

Well, is religion redundant now? Has human nature become utterly different since the modern scientific and industrial movement began about 200 years ago? I do not think so. A good deal of religion survives; public-opinion polls show that 75 per cent of the British people say that they believe in God, and over 90 per cent want to continue religious education in the nation's schools. And although the institutions of religion have been shaken badly by the wind of change, as I look around the world in 1969, I see everywhere attempts to find substitutes for the old religious traditions. I see Communism, which is a kind of religion with Marx or Lenin or Stalin or Mao or the Party in place of a god, with the dream of a perfect society in place of heaven. I see Nationalism, which has often called for a religious self-sacrifice, human sacrifice to the god of patriotism. I see the younger generation putting its religious energy into protests against the wars and injustice and material and spiritual poverty in our world. I live among students, and most of them run a mile from the thought of the organised Church or the official-looking parson; but I observe that many of these students are rejecting the materialism which religious believers also reject. And isn't there something valid in this contempt among intelligent young people for the exploitation of sex in commercial advertising or for the rat race of commercial life? Isn't sex or money often worshipped in adult society as a substitute for God? Would you say that we in Britain have largely escaped from the illusions of Communism, or Nationalism, or student protest, or obsessive sex, or money-making? Perhaps so; but would you go on to say that we in Britain have no need to be worried about the condition of our society? Aren't there many signs both of a basic cynicism and of a search for something which we could feel deeply in our emotions and serve in our lives?

No, materialism of the kind which we have had for some time now is shown up by history as inadequate for human nature, and many people in Britain are waking up to this fact. The climate of opinion is beginning to change, I think, and there is indeed beginning to be a danger of uncontrolled emotionalism becoming the popular attitude, at least in the younger generation. If religion is cut out, then a gap is left in the human spirit, and the spiritual problem of man is how to fill that gap. So only the ignorant or the silly despise religion's attempt to meet a human need.

Many thoughtful unbelievers would, I know, agree with much in that estimate of the spiritual vacuum which exists for many in Britain now. But finally I want to say that to me, and to millions of my fellow-believers within our minority, religious faith is not a series of empty, meaningless words as it often seems to unbelievers. Faith rests on experience, for it is experience that teaches us where to put our trust. Nothing is more important than this: we should realise that religious faith is not pretending to believe silly things. Amid the mysteries of human life, it is knowing where to put your trust. I became a believer because I admired some people who were believers. They looked towards God; most of them weren't saints, but their whole lives were given a pattern and a purpose because they were directed towards that mystery, and that mystery was clearly a reality to them. There was 'something in them'. That made me think, and the feeling that there might be something valid in the religious quest gripped me. And so I set out on the journey for myself. I found that it wasn't like science, except that in religion as in science you have to be humble. It was more like a political enthusiasm such as Communism or Nationalism. It was, I found, more like the young student's vision of a world made new and beautiful and just and friendly. And above all, religion was, I found, like a marriage.

Arguing with an unbeliever is a bit like an argument in a pub between a married man and a hardened bachelor who objects to the loss of freedom, the expense, and the hard work. Yes, religion is like marriage: as demanding as that, as much of a discipline as that, as full of problems and ecstasies and enjoyment, as strong in a quiet happiness which nothing in the world can take away, as fascinating in its continuous revelation of another person, as rewarding in its development of a mature love. A faith, like a marriage, is the heart of a strong religion, and it can survive the disappearance of a familiar background, as when a man and his wife move their home. Only this kind of religious faith will survive strongly in the period into which we are moving.

2. GOD IN AN AGE OF HUMANISM

I KNOW from the people I live with, I know from my own experience, that the modern sense of technical mastery and economic progress can result in a new pride in being human. We can do so many more things than our fathers could do. We have so many more opportunities opening out before us. There is a thrill of being alive in 1969. 'Glory to man in the highest, and on earth prosperity!' So what has religion got to do with this new humanism? At first sight, it seems to many that religion is the enemy. Enter progress – exit God. But look more closely!

It is a thought-provoking fact that many of the pioneers in modern science were religious believers. Often they disagreed with some of the teachings of the churches at the time; and this produced some tragic conflicts between them and the religious authorities. But it is a fact of history that many of them worshipped God as Christians. They regarded nature as 'a second Bible', in which the Creator's thoughts were written, and they regarded science as 'thinking the Creator's thoughts after him.' It meant everything to them that we live in an orderly universe. Up the telescope and down the microscope they found the beauty of order, and they believed that this was because the universe had been created by God. They were not ashamed to spend their time investigating tiny little bits of the creation, precisely because it was the creation, the work of God. On the other hand, they did not worship nature;

they did not regard it as too sacred to investigate or as too perfect to disturb, because the Creator in whom they believed was thought by them to be beyond as well as within nature. He alone in his eternity was truly sacred, fully perfect, and so it was right to be curious and even masterful in one's approach to the universe which he had made. Indeed, God had given reason and power to man in order that man should be curious and masterful. Here, you see, we have a picture of God not as the enemy, not as the emperor who overpowers little men, but as the friend and fellow-worker who delights to see men exercising the abilities which he has given them.

I believe that this is the picture of God which we need to recover in our time; and I know that this kind of attitude is in fact already widespread among Christian theologians and preachers. A pride in being human, a pride in being clever and capable, based upon a pride in being the adult children of God: that is a pride which I find in much Christian teaching during the twentieth century – although the older attitude of putting the main emphasis on man's immaturity and sense of failure and guilt does linger on, encouraged by the wars and the other disasters of our century. I believe that the Christian way of dealing with the facts of human failure and guilt is not to harp on the littleness of man: on the contrary, the wise Christian treats the misery of man as itself a revelation of his grandeur. That phrase which I have just used is an echo of Pascal, the seventeenth-century mathematician. I mean by it that when we fail to reach our targets it is because we set ourselves targets beyond our strength; we have the greatness to do that, and our failure shows that we are a mixture of strength and weakness. And when we feel guilty, it is basically because we are haunted by the conviction that we are not meant to fail, for it is our destiny to reach those targets. The twentieth century has been a period when we or our fathers have swung so very rapidly from pride to despair, from confidence to anxiety, from achievement to guilt. Surely in the last quarter of this century the pendulum ought to come to rest with an understanding of human nature as a mixture.

Why do I think that a really mature understanding of the mysteries of man's own nature ought to include the faith that God makes man and works with him?

As a student of the story of the twentieth century, I know how very easy it is to try to make man less than human, if you operate with a humanism which does not include any religious dimension. The history of our time is stuffed full of the disasters which follow. In my last talk I said that the materialism which is widespread today fails to satisfy the hunger of man for things other than consumer goods. Aren't some industrial disputes basically protests against the attitude that his pay is all that matters to a worker? Yet the modern substitutes for religion also dehumanise man. Communism crushes the freedom of man for the sake of a political slogan. Nationalism cuts man down into being a mere citizen or a mere soldier. Youthful idealism, shouting for a revolution, forgets that no revolution in history fails to persecute because no revolution is patient with the awkward individual. The worship of sex turns every women into just a body, as the worship of money turns every home into just a collection of furniture. And these tendencies are already present in countries rich in material wealth.

Many scientists are, I find, extremely worried about what may happen unless the advance of our knowledge and technical skills is stripped of its careless arrogance. For these scientists know that it will take more than their abilities to stop the destruction of the city by selfishness in transport and housing and living, to stop the division of the world into affluent and hungry, to stop the exhaustion of the earth's natural resources, and to stop the use of nuclear and biological and chemical weapons. Will the solution of these problems, so sickeningly familiar to us, be found in the development of a truly scientific understanding of man in society? Many young people are turning from natural science to social science in the hope that these problems, which concern them deeply, can be answered by a growth of knowledge; and of course I too agree that psychologists and sociologists and other experts can help very greatly to cure us of our follies. But I note that little of the wisdom which we need has yet been produced by these experts; and I note also that usually in history, when they hesitated to think of other human beings as mere producers or consumers or as mere members of a class or a nation or as mere bodies or brains, it has been because of a belief in man with a religious dimension. It is possible that science may save us; but if the sense of religious mystery no longer surrounds humanism, if the sense of religious obligation no longer disciplines our selfishness, I (for one) believe that the suicide of civilisation is probable.

Man, I observe, has been regarded as sacred when man has been regarded as a son of God. As a Christian, I am proud that my religion teaches the highest humanism possible. Karl Barth, the very biblical, very orthodox Swiss theologian who died last December, loved to use a very daring phrase: 'the humanity of God.' By that he meant that there is a real kinship between God and man, and that this family likeness was revealed to us when God used the human nature of Jesus Christ as he did. That view should be contrasted with the teaching of Sigmund Freud, for example. Freud taught that human nature is really controlled by selfish, animal appetites, so that it will always be at odds with the civilisation which is necessary if people are to live together and develop skills. Furthermore, Freud taught that this human nature is the highest life which exists in the real world, so that it is a mere illusion to think that the reality which surrounds our life is like a parent. 'Reality' is indifferent or hostile to the needs of man. Out there it is cold, and we go into the dark. You will see now why I claim that Christianity is the highest humanism. Christianity says: your human dignity arises from your creation by God; your spiritual nature is different from the other animals (although we now know that your life has evolved from animal life) – it is different because it is more Godlike; your real needs are supplied by the reality which surrounds you, and your best dreams are supported by the reality which throws everlasting arms beneath you; you in your personal history are gripped and held forever by that reality; you are made not only to produce or fight or copulate or research and die but also to be part of the eternal joy of God.

I cannot prove to you now that this Christian faith in God and man is true. It is faith, a trust, produced by Christian experience, just as Freudianism was a lack of trust, produced by Freud's experience. What I can do – what I hope I have now done – is to explain why Christians regard this faith as the most important contribution which they can offer to the discussion about the nature and crisis of man.

3. CHRIST IN AN AGE OF CRITICISM

IN MY first two talks I tried to suggest that religious faith is still a worthwhile activity, although this is, on the whole, an age of materialism. I tried to say also that the Christian understanding of the dignity of man is worth consideration in a time when so many who are dissatisfied by materialism are asking what man, what humanism, really is. But so far I have only hinted at the crux of the matter, which is the question of who Christ is for us today. I am sure that Christianity – the whole colossal organisation, all the art, architecture, music, and literature, the whole emotional fact which covers the prayers and lives of thousands of millions of human beings, including many of the best who have ever prayed or lived – all this Christianity depends on the figure of one who lived as a Jew for just over thirty years just over 1,900 years ago; who died, and is said to be alive in some sense now. Christianity is about Christ, and were Christ to be pushed out of his dominant position we should need a new religion.

Let us face the fact that the figure of Christ has been obscured for many people by the modern atmosphere. The method of scientific investigation has been applied to the great story of this man. This tough-minded approach has compared him with other religious leaders, and has emphasised that the

Jesus of history was a man of Palestine in a period remote from our own. The angels around him seem to fly away. Reports of miracles performed by him seem to be legends, at least in some cases; and it seems difficult to recover the detailed history behind the stories which may have some truth in them. The words of Jesus reach us only through the Christians, and his teaching, so far as it can be recovered, seems strange to our world when we look at it carefully, for it was teaching about 'the coming of the Kingdom of God.' Jesus and his first followers seem to have expected the Kingdom of God to come dramatically, completely, and quickly. It did not come like that. You are not to be blamed if you ask: What, then, does the teaching mean today? Ours is an age of criticism. Christ has not escaped criticism. Christians cannot escape the consequences.

We are, I think, in the middle of a great unsettlement in Christianity: the criticism of the New Testament is only a part of this. For centuries Christians believed that a fairly complete system of doctrines about God, man, and the universe was taught by Christ to his disciples and handed on from generation to generation. The Church taught this system, and the Bible proved it. Of course Christ was infallible because he was God, and in one way or another the Church and the Bible shared Christ's freedom from error. This general picture of a Christianity ready-made, and guaranteed in its details, was accepted by almost everyone, although people differed, often violently, about precisely which bits of the picture, which doctrines or rules, required the strongest emphasis. Now we are not nearly so certain about where the authority lies in Christianity; we are witnessing, in fact, the slow but steady decline and fall of Christian dogmatism.

But I think that what is essential in Christianity's faith in Christ can survive in an age of criticism – as Christianity can survive, although materialism and a secular humanism attack its faith in God. Let me now state briefly what I think we can honestly and reasonably say about Jesus Christ. It does not amount to an elaborate system of doctrine. But it is enough.

He was real, a carpenter who was crucified, a rabbi and more than a rabbi, a prophet and more than a prophet, a teacher who taught a clear message. This message was that God was about to show himself as King on earth as in heaven. Some of that message Jesus shared with other Jews of the period who nursed apocalyptic hopes: hopes that God would reveal who was who. But the centre of the message of Jesus did not rest on any prediction about the date or the method of the coming of God's Kingdom. The centre rested on the faith that God was King – God was real, and he was ruler – and above all God was Father, good beyond the goodness of our fathers on earth. Nor was the coming of God's Kingdom thought of as belonging only to the future. God's Kingdom was beginning in the life and work of Jesus himself. Jesus claimed that the future would be an unfolding of that work, and so he commanded men and women to leave all and join the work.

All reasonable criticism of the New Testament does, I think, leave this account of Jesus still standing. And it leaves also standing the fact that, although Jesus was put to death for disturbing the political and religious establishment of the day, after his death many Christians have experienced his life and power carrying on in them. Whatever happened to the body of Jesus after his death, his spirit certainly made an overwhelming impact on his friends who had been grief-stricken; the faith and life and power of the Christians rose, and that to me is the deepest meaning of the miracle of Easter. The Christian Church, the fellowship of those who have risen over the great tragedy of the cross, is the living body of Christ at work in the world, from century to century. And it is a further fact of history that this fellowship has been amazingly creative in relating the life of Jesus the carpenter, the teaching of Jesus the rabbi, to a great variety of situations. In the New Testament we can watch it happening, as Paul and John very boldly related the life of Christ to the life of the Greek world. It has happened again and again: in the Middle Ages in Europe, at the Protestant Reformation, in recent Catholicism, in the expansion of Christianity as the only really world-wide religion in history. In America, in Africa, in Asia, in factories and laboratories, the life of Jesus Christ has gone on, his spirit has won its victories. Christianity has been very flexible, but there has been this continuity: the impact of the spirit of Christ. Terrible things have been done in the name of Christ, and our critical spirit can help us to avoid trying to defend the whole of the history of Christians. Christianity is very far from being the perfect religion. But the history of Christ is there, and I believe that this central drama ought to be defended as unique in the story of mankind. This is not a dogma – it is a drama before our eyes. No other man has had anything like this influence and this achievement in bringing millions nearer to God the King and God the Father. I do not like discussing the nature of Jesus Christ in terms of Greek philosophy, or in any other abstract terms, but I do find it completely honest – and completely necessary – to say the one thing that is essential to Christian faith: that in Jesus Christ, yesterday and today, God has acted in order to show himself as King and Father.

What, then, are we to think about Christ? Mainly, it is a moral or spiritual question. All too often we Christians try to keep Jesus Christ in a world of mythology, because in the real world, in history, in flesh among us, his message would be disturbingly relevant. And I feel guilty because I am unable to show convincingly what the message of Jesus Christ for you is. I know that I am not alone in feeling disturbed by this figure who still fascinates us. The consciences of many Christians are troubled nowadays, and there is a ferment of thought about what Christ means. This is confusing and uncomfortable, but it is better than the previous tendency to identify Christ's strange commands with the conventional morality of the white middle classes. One of the harsh truths that is coming home to us is that Christ is against the division of mankind into nations which threaten each other with war. Another harsh truth is that Christ is against the imprisonment of two-thirds of mankind in poverty under the threat of famine, while the privileged of the earth get more affluent and more bored. Yet the Gospel of Christ for us today is more awkward, and more mysterious, than a programme of social reform. What Christ is most against is our smug pride, and his Gospel disturbs us in the depths. To our complacency it holds up that vision of life as it might be, in the 'impossible possibilities' of the Sermon on the Mount. To our compromising worldliness it holds up the blinding vision of God.

No, I can't say clearly what Christ means to you. But I can say this: that after all our criticism applied to the records about him, he strides towards us out of the pages of the book, and he, more than any other man who has lived, comes into the twentieth century as our critic and our judge.

4. THE CHURCH IN AN AGE OF REVOLUTION

THE CHURCH does not seem to be at home in our age of revolution. In an age of material prosperity for many people in the richer countries of the world, the priests and preachers do not seem to be really with the new democracy. In an age of new technical achievement the Church seems to look backwards in thought and life. In an age which is critical of the past, the Church seems to belong to the past. And we must add Christianity's biggest problems all over Asia and Africa today: in an age of freedom, the Church seems to be identified with colonialism; in an age of hunger, the Church seems to be identified with the privileged white minority of mankind. Here is a formidable list of problems for the Church, and some response must be made to the challenge, for no religion can flourish except in a religious community which flourishes, putting the beliefs of that religion into action and passing them on to the new generation and to adult inquirers.

What response do I make, as a member of the Christian Church? Well, the main thing I find I want to say to myself and to my fellow-churchmen is: *hold on.* I believe that the Church, despite its confusion and depression, is today the principle custodian of mankind's spiritual heritage. In an age of materialism the Church has to keep alive a vision of life as something more than producing and consuming, and a trust in life as a spiritual discovery of greater and greater goodness and joy – life being rather like a successful marriage. In an age of proud humanism which is constantly invaded by a sense of despair about man's true position in the universe, the Church has to keep on saying: man's real greatness lies in the likeness and the contact between the spirit of man and the spirit of the eternal God. In an age which knows that its spiritual life does not match its technical achievement, the Church has to keep alive the teachings and examples of the great masters of the spiritual life, and, particularly, the Church has to be in some sense a continuation of the life of the one and only Jesus Christ.

I am proud to belong to a Church which is in fact quietly doing these things, for all its faults, around the world today. And I am compelled to say that if the Christian Church were to abandon these duties, there would be nothing to replace it. Do you think that the British Humanist Association would replace it? Do you think that any of the other religions in the world – each undergoing a crisis of modernisation far more serious than Christianity's – would succeed in providing a faith for the future? I do not wish to sneer at the British Humanist Association's small membership (its recruiting problems are worse than the Church's), and I do not wish to attack any other religion (modern life is attacking them more effectively than the most fanatical Christian missionary), but as one who is inside the Christian Church I want to say that at a time of very great difficulty this is still a good place to be.

Hold on then if, like me, you belong to the Christian tradition. And, I want to add, thank God that Christianity in the twentieth century is still showing many signs of its astonishing and unique power to connect its tradition with a new situation. Almost every branch of the Church is today budding, and some are blossoming, with ideas and experiments. The

Church has been pruned, certainly; it has lost millions of nominal adherents who were attached to it in the days of its power, and more tragically a lot of thoughtful people have dropped off because they did not think it honest to remain fully connected with the old-fashioned Church. So apart from the United States of America (where church-going has enjoyed a boom for the last twenty-five years), the Christian Church is everywhere a minority. This minority is depressed and confused, or is often tempted to be so. But look more closely and you will see the battle between faith in the future and the forces of inertia and defeatism. In Asia and Africa you will see a Church rooting itself in the life of a free nation. In the Roman Catholic Church there is a modernisation in worship, there is a ferment in theology, which fifteen years ago no one expected. In the Anglican and Protestant Churches you will find some things equally surprising. Those who question the traditional ways of expressing the Christian faith have not been shouted down; on the contrary, prominent church leaders have spoken out in sympathy. The old methods of organisation are being overhauled extensively, and the search for Christian unity is leading church members to re-examine a whole host of emotional prejudices and practical problems. In villages, suburbs, housing estates and city centres small congregations are being renewed as they come together week by week in a deeper fellowship and, above all, as they go out together in service to the neighbourhood and in concern for the world – and millions of individual Christians *are* going to work in the modern world. Many nurses, many teachers, many of the people who staff the welfare state, many of the people who are doing something about world poverty – many of these people are Christians, a higher proportion than you would expect in these days of small congregations.

I am sure that the weakness of the Christian Church can be exaggerated – by critics who do not know enough about its life today, or by Christians who are too romantic about the past in comparison with the present. The true history of the Church has been the story of a minority in every age, for only the minority has ever taken an active part in the deeper, spiritual life of the Church. Today the Christian minority is still as courageous as it has ever been, perhaps more so. Do you want to see moral courage? Many brave men and women have been recruited for the noble army of martyrs in our time, more than in any previous century, and often they have blessed their persecutors. Do you want to see intellectual courage? Well, our century has produced not only vigorous theology but also careful, chastened, responsible theology.

But we all know that if the Church is to stay afloat as it should in the stormy seas of this age of revolution, and if the Church is to be any kind of *QE2*, a floating home for mankind as we cross the ocean to a new world, then what is now going on in the Church is not enough. We do need a new power, like the power which has driven the Church through many a crisis in the past. Christians, I find, usually agree that we need a new Reformation in our time, and I would myself put it more strongly than that: we need a new Whitsun to give the Church an excitement, a bubbling joy, an assurance, a community in the Spirit, and we need a new Paul and a new John to give us the theology for an age of science. So I find myself driven to say one thing more, as I end this series of talks.

In the old days of church history, when there was a crisis like this, they said to each other, they said it behind locked doors in Jerusalem or in the catacombs under Rome, they said it long ago when the heathen pirates invaded Christian England, they said it in a jungle village or in China when a mob howled for the blood of a missionary, they said it in concentration camps under Hitler or Stalin, they said the words which seem so stale in more comfortable days, so churchy, so dull; they said – *let us pray*. I say that now, to myself and to any who long for a new gift of the Holy Spirit of God to the Christian Church in our time. But there is a way of praying which belongs peculiarly to our time, which is a time of an increasingly educated democracy in the Church as elsewhere. It is prayer in a group, prayer after hard thought, prayer after free discussion, prayer leading into vigorous action. All over the world now there are groups which are like this or which are trying to grow like this. But we do not have enough. Nothing is more important than this. Let many of the buildings fall down, let many of the committees bury themselves under all that paper, if only you have more groups like this. For some, such a group must be the Christian family itself, in the home; or the group of friends in a hospital ward. But if you are free to go out to work and to meet others, who is the neighbour with whom you should start a group tomorrow?

Such a group would have as its chief concern not the perfection of the individual's piety but this even more difficult aim: to see amid the confusion where God is already acting, to spot how he moves his left hand when we thought that only his right hand mattered, to acknowledge that he keeps on visiting his people, to watch the new thing he is doing in the world which is coming to birth (and in our old churches also), to mark his quick steps in all the rapid change around us, to listen to the wind of the Spirit blowing through a tired history, to obey and to work with him where his action is. Our groups need to be groups at the disposal of our God; for our God is acting faster than we Christians are, as he goes towards the time when all that he wants will be done by all mankind. The Church of this living, revolutionary God ought to be at home in an age of revolution.